COLLECTIONS

A Harcourt Reading / Language Arts Program

PHONICS PRACTICE READERS

Harcourt

Orlando   Boston   Dallas   Chicago   San Diego

Visit *The Learning Site!*
www.harcourtschool.com

CONTENTS

Monkey

by Laura Edwards

Illustrations by Holly Cooper

monkey

mop

mask

motorcycle

milk

I Am

by Virginia Parker Illustrations by Shawn Banner

 I am a cat.

I am a rabbit.

I am a squirrel.

I am a butterfly.

I am a duck.

I am a girl.

Sam the Seal

by Laura Edwards

Illustrations by
Scott Scheidly

Sam

22

I am Sam.

I am a seal.

I am Sam.

I am a star.

Sam

by
Mary Louise Novak

Illustrations by
Marsha Slomowitz

I am Sam.

Sam sat.

I am Sam.

Sam sat.

I am Sam.

Sam sat.

Ssss!

WHERE IS CAT?

by Isabel Paz

Illustrations by Julia Gorton

Where is Cat?

Meow.

Cat? Cat?

40

Meow.

Cat?

Cat?

43

Here, Cat!

Pat

by Ruby Mae
Illustrations by Rick Kirkman

Look, Pat!

Tap! Tap!

Here, Pat!

Tap! Tap!

Come, Pat!

Tap! Tap!

Pat!

by Ruby Mae

Illustrations by Deborah Melmon

Look at the ham.

Look at the egg.

Hap has the ham.

Hap has the egg.

Hap has the pan.

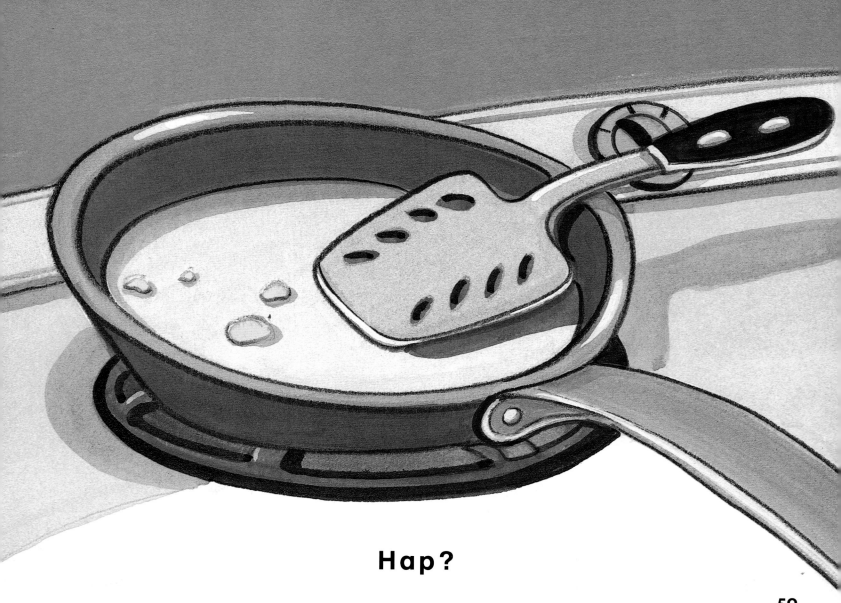

Hap?

Mmmm.

That Cat!

by Mary Louise Novak

Illustrations by
Holly Cooper

Dad had the cookies.

Mmmm, good!

Tad had the pan.

That cat!

Dad is mad.

Come, Tad!

Good cat.

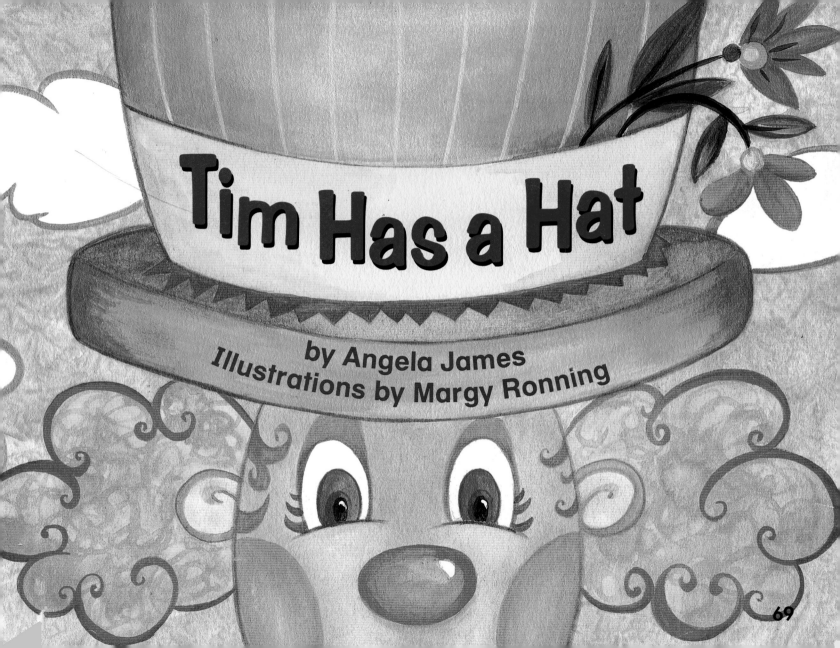

Tim Has a Hat

by Angela James
Illustrations by Margy Ronning

Here is Tim.

Tim has a hat.

Tim tips his hat.

Tim sits on his hat.

Tim is sad.

Where is his hat?

Wow! Here it is!

The Nap

by Kristie Porraro

Illustrations by Donald Saaf

Can Dog nap?

Dog can nap.

Can cat nap?

Cat can nap, too.

Dog has a pan.

Cat has a pan, too.

Good dog!
Good cat!

What a Kick!

by Robert Fletcher
Illustrations by Michael Chesworth

Mick can kick.

I can not kick.

Good kick, Mick!

I can not kick.

That is a big kick.

Now Mick is sad.

Here it is, Mick!

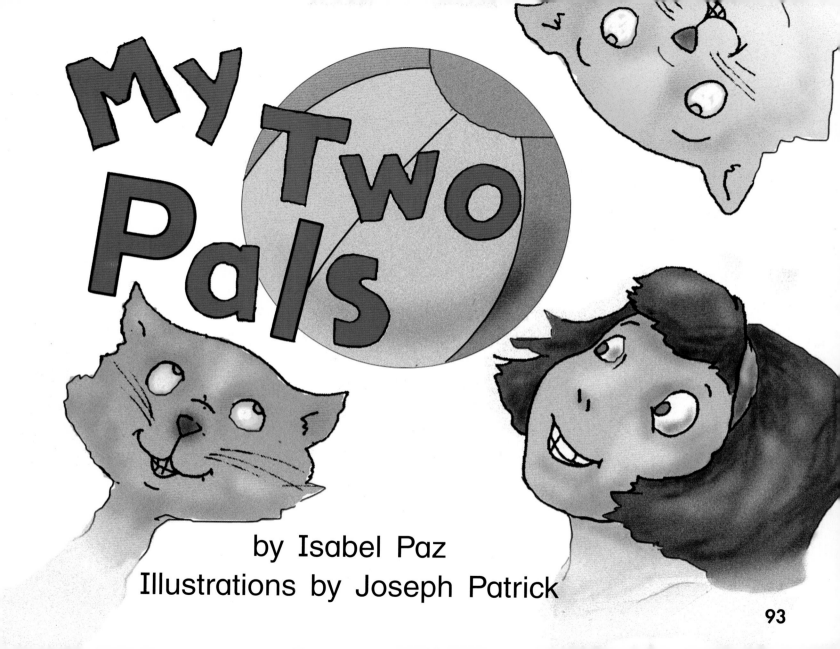

My Two Pals

by Isabel Paz

Illustrations by Joseph Patrick

Sal is sad.

Dad has Al.

Will you lick my hand?

Will you sit on my lap?

Dad has Hal.

Sal has two cat pals.

Wow! Two cat pals
for me!

Come All!

by Megan Casey

Illustrations by
Michael Letzig

103

105